THE ULTIMATE
STEP-BY-STEP
GUIDE TO YOUR
SPIRITUAL AWAKENING

WRITTEN BY

Dayna Marten

Copyright

Dedication

To my daughter, Nicole. You are the root that grounds me. Without your inspiration, none of this would be possible. You keep me on course and are the wind beneath my wings.

To my son, Brandon. You are the reason that I dream big. Your unending optimism and old soul push me onward every day to do better, be better, and live outside the box.

To my mom, Jennifer. Your life has meaning and purpose. You chose to be my mom, and Universal Order has been fulfilled through you. Thank you for my life.

Contents

Introduction

Life does not have to be a struggle. You have all the tools necessary to live a peaceful and fulfilling life, you just don't know it yet. Walk with me through the sequenced steps of your awakening and let me guide you towards the path of your best and highest good. You are so important, you have purpose, your life has meaning, and your journey is important to Universal Order.

Preface

What IS a spiritual awakening? When the reality that you have always known begins to fade and a new internal understanding begins to emerge that compels you to observe and process the physical world around you in a new way. You begin to question everything you thought you knew as reality. You begin to see the eternal, never-ending trajectory of your soul's journey, and walking this path becomes your only desire. You can't help yourself, you can't control the compulsion to learn everything and anything about this new way of thinking, and you desire nothing more than to be in alignment with your soul path. The objective becomes to merge your soul with your human experience.

This book is a step-by-step instructional tool for unboxing your soul so you can find your true self. It is the ultimate guide to navigate your way through your awakening. It is designed to help you find your way out of the box that oppresses your true being, to free your mind, and free your soul. I will take you step by step through the process of awakening, with an overview of why you are awakening, and then a dive into deep spiritual pontifications, concept by concept, with advice and instructions to ensure success in this journey, and the next.

I'm very honored to convey this information to you and I'm excited about your new journey!

Chapter 1

Your Ancient Self:

Who You Have Always Been

Whether you are 99 or 19, what would you tell your past self if you could? What would you warn against, and what would you advocate for? Think about it for a minute. How many decisions in your life were made from a deep, peaceful, meaningful place of knowing, absolutely, what was in your best interest at the time?

Alternatively, how many of your life choices were made in a place of hopeful doubt? Doing it despite your intuition, forgoing that check deep in your gut because whatever it was at the time, is what you wanted at the moment; only to have it unravel over time, and in the end, regretfully wishing you would have listened to yourself (and maybe even others).

Let's explore your ancient self and get to know the piece of you that knows all things in infinite wisdom... let me take you on a journey to meet your soul, your ancient self, the never ending you - who you have infinitely been.

Navigating life can be a bit of a struggle at times, and quite honestly, it's literally sink or swim. You either "make it" or you don't. Sometimes it seems like endless swimming, endless treading in the mud of life. Believe it or not, it doesn't have to be this way. There is a better way, the way you were originally wired to experience life. You are equipped with every tool you need to live a productive, happy, and peaceful life. We all have it within us, it's our internal compass.

It's called your intuition, and I guarantee every mistake that you've made in your life came from ignoring it, and every good aspect of your life came from following it. Your intuition is your ancient soul speaking to your consciousness trying to point you towards your True North. Your soul, working along with signs, synchronicities, and your inner knowings, is your life compass. The same soul that was here before you took your first breath, the same soul that will pick up when you die, is the exact same soul that tries to guide you today. That same soul, your ancient self, lives within you now, and it knows where you came from, it knows what's on the other side of all this, and it is trying to lead you to your best and highest good, according to Universal Order.

Your name is written in the Book of Life, you are a beautiful thread in the tapestry of Universal Order. You are stitched together by the agape love of Source energy, and YOU are never-ending. Your soul has existed eternally, you have existed eternally, and here, in this flesh and bone experience, you have a job to do. Your awakening is your soul finally breaking through the box of your mind to do what you came here to do.

It chose (you chose) to come here for either a special mission, or correction via repeat (possibly on a mission of correction), but many have lost their way, forgotten their purpose, trapped in the box of life, enamored by the deliciousness of the physical experience. If you feel that you are being called to return to your roots, to dig deeper into the who, what, where, when, and why of this crazy thing called life, if you are awakening... the following chapters contain everything you need to know to progress successfully in your journey.

Chapter 2

The Mission:

What Is This All About?

First and foremost, you must understand that you are a soul having a human experience, not a human having a soul experience. We are all here to live a life of peace and experience this leg of our eternal soul's journey in a state of understanding and exploration, not fear and anxiety. We have missions of purpose. There are planters, waterers, tenders, and harvesters amongst us, all doing our part to expand the human consciousness and awaken souls to the true purpose of their journey. We are ALL warriors here to help other souls to find their way home.

You are awakening now because humanity needs you. We are alive, right here, right now, in a time of massive transformation for humanity. You have a part to play and a job to do. Now is the time to break free from the box and do what you came here to do during this time of the collective Great Awakening aka The Age of Aquarius. Your soul is restless, set it free. You are here, reading this book right now for one of two reasons - you are either here to guide others through the Great Awakening, or you are here to elevate your understanding to the point where you CAN guide others through the Great Awakening. The awakening from the deep slumber of a soulless, mechanical life, plugged into the Matrix of the reality in your mind that has been designed (programmed) to keep you on the trajectory of internal failure. An awakening from the deception meant to keep you asleep so you don't complete your mission and the cycle of disparity can continue.

The longer we slumber in apathy, the longer the machine behind the scenes prospers. The machine behind the scenes is the oppositional force that continuously suppresses and oppresses your immense personal power... through apathy to your condition.

It keeps you dumbed down so you do not know that you can do incredible things. It keeps you apathetic through the modeling of what a good life is "supposed" to be through TV, movies, and social media that cause dissatisfaction in your life by compelling you to compare your life to the fantasy lives that you see on the screens (ask yourself why tv shows are called "programs"). It is, among other things, the poisoning of our minds and our bodies, to cause mental and physical disease so you will die before your mission is even attempted and the darkness can never be illuminated. Your awakening is a serious threat to the design of this planet.

It is the dogma of organized religions and the institutions of education that keep you from knowing your soul and controlling your own thoughts. This social engineering is the framework of the box that you are enclosed in. Social engineering is staging the situations and circumstances to obtain a desired collective outcome of low vibrational weakness and apathy. Ask yourself why you are being prompted, manipulated, to act in a certain way, and for what purpose?

Your mission during your awakening is to find your soul by peeling away the layers of deception that have become your reality, so you can not only find your soul, but to help others find their souls as well. It is literally a chain of awakenings. Each of us is a catalyst to the next... I'm passing the torch to you, and you will grow to the point where you will eventually pass the torch to another - in whatever way is meaningful to them; and so forth and so on until we are all awakened to our true purpose.

My job, my soul mission, the purpose of MY life, is to help you with your initial awakening. I will guide you through the transformation from flesh to soul, and prepare you for the next leg of your journey, for whatever part you will play in the Great Awakening. If what I say here resonates with you, then know that this is what you need to know right now. If what I say here pokes you in a sore spot, you may want to look a little deeper as to why. If you get angry, go deep inside and ask yourself why. Take what you will and leave the rest. It'll be here when you're ready.

Let's begin by introducing you to your own soul. You see, your soul was in existence long before you took your first breath in this meat suit, and it will be here long after the ol' meat suit finally wears out. It is eternal energy, and it is the essence of who you are, the threads that YOU are sewn from.

YOU are eternal energy. Physical science says that energy cannot be created nor destroyed, it simply transitions from one form to another. In this human experience, your essence, your soul, and your energy, is animated in your skin and bones and expressed through your inner knowings, intuition, and synchronicities. If you are a funny person, you have eternally been funny. If you are a very serious person, you have been eternally serious. The fundamentals of your person have always been and will always be.

The objective in this human experience is to find that ancient soul, your true self, and mesh it with the animated reality of being alive so it can lead you and guide you to the path of your best highest good; so you can live a purposeful and peaceful life focusing on your soul's mission versus the mechanical execution of just simply being alive inside the safety of the box that has engineered your human experience.

The ancient soul that existed before your physical body, the ancient soul that will be here to pick up where you leave off when the body finally wears out, is the exact same soul that co-exists with your consciousness right now. That same ancient soul speaks to you. That soul knows where you came from, what you are supposed to be doing right now, and where you're headed when this adventure is over. If you will find it and allow it to guide you, it will ALWAYS lead you to the path of your best and highest good.

Chapter 3

The Box: Your Human Experience

When a person can't find a deep sense of meaning,
they distract themselves with pleasure."

~ Viktor Frankl

In this short 100-year physical existence, that same
soul, your soul, lives within your body and
communicates to you through your intuition, signs
and synchronicities in your life. It always points you
toward the path of your best and highest good. Your
all-knowing ancient self that you have forgotten, or
more exactly been conditioned to suppress throughout

your life, is readily available to show you the way to a purposeful, rewarding, peaceful life.

During your human life, your mind, your identity, is molded from birth to fit into the box that contains the preconceived expectations of who you are, given to you by the situations and circumstances of those to whom you were born to. Your gender, the color of your hair, the color of your skin, who your parents are, where they live, what they do for a living, their socioeconomic status, what their beliefs and experiences are (including all of their baggage), culture, religion, education, society.

These are all the labels and expectations that you did not choose but are bound to fulfill by being born into it. Going against these dogmas is difficult, leading to more box labels - rebellious, uncooperative, and disappointing to name a few. Life just becomes easier if you just do what you are told to do and be what you are expected to be. This is reinforced repeatedly through traditions, culture, religion, family, and society. It is constantly morphing our path and our purpose; and burying the soul that must frustratingly transverse the path of your limited and frail human understanding.

"I must obey my family, my culture, my traditions, my religion; must push forward, must get more, must work harder to get more, must get recognition, must have validation, must be redeemed, must continue to feed the social machine with the expectations that have been set forth since my birth - and if I don't I will face despair, failure, rejection, disappointment, poverty, and societal judgment".

The expectations assigned to you will dictate your whole existence before you even have a chance to know who you truly are... and the soul gets buried, pushed down, and dampened to the point that it is forgotten. This is why the human experience is a struggle. Rebellious children trying to make their way in a world that wants to consume them as a resource to perpetuate the motion of the machine... a machine that runs on fear, desperation, confusion, and despair.

Out of our herd mentality is birthed a compliant human existence where our internal desires and knowings are displaced by a desire to meet these expectations for fear of rudimentary rejection. Assuming your position in life, and being what is expected of you, is much easier than not, and thus begins the blind and empty journey of the human struggle. The white-knuckle grip on success and achievement, whatever that means for you (and the disappointment of not achieving it) becomes the objective. The cycle never ends, with the constant reproduction of offspring that are now subjected to the same box that you live in.

Over and over again, generation after generation from birth to death we walk in the confusing emptiness of our physicality with no regard as to why we are all here doing this. It doesn't have to be like this. We have the tools to live in a better way.

Chapter 4

The Walking Dead:
The Blind Leading the Blind

Assuming that it is agreed that the body without the soul is dead, then the separation of the soul from the body is death. Thus, most of us are the walking dead - because most of us have no understanding of the importance of our soul's journey in this animated state of being alive. The true essence of who you are is buried beneath the oppression of expectations.

You are ushered into this "aliveness" through the portal of your mother's womb, and at that moment, you are divided into two separate components - the flesh and bone body that is ruled by your consciousness, and the eternal soul that resides within your subconscious. Young children inherently combine the two until they are taught by the world system (via parents and institutions) not to.

To add insult to injury, the physical body is subject to an expiration date, which adds to the anxious pursuit of accomplishment. A 100-year box of a timeline, if you're lucky, and for the first 20 years or so most aren't even conscious of their own power... so you have 80 years, maybe, to achieve all the things we are supposed to achieve and meet all the expectations that you are supposed to fulfill, according to the box that defines our identity. We are taught, from childhood to mechanically concede to these expectations, boxed into these 100 years of frantic achievement, clinging to the accomplishments defined by human society as "a good life".

Most will live and die in this box that is designed to keep you so busy that you never contemplate why you are doing any of these things. All the while, as we traverse the expected path of obedience - education, religion, career, family, house, children, we all have an inner voice that tries to lead and guide us through the maze of life, but it is consistently overridden by the desire to follow our own free will.

Each step, each page, each chapter of your life leads to the next, constantly ongoing – even after death. That inner voice is your ancient self, poking and prodding you in the direction of what your life should be to experience this adventure in the best possible way. Your ancient self knows the path, while your human self is lost in a maze of overwhelming choices and decisions.

This inner knowing, this internal guidance system, is showing you the direction of your soul's journey - but often the flesh nature, the ego of the human, the meat suit coping mechanism, wants what it wants - when it wants it - and overrides the internal compass to get it. This is the separation of your soul from your body, hence the Walking Dead.

Until you meet the objective of reuniting your soul with your consciousness, combining your conscious experience with your subconscious guidance, you will remain The Walking Dead.

Chapter 5

The Big Hoax:

What They Need You to Believe

Most of us inherently know that there is something way more profound than the existence we are living. We know it, we feel it, and are compelled to acknowledge it. Thus, many of us cling to the safety of religion to make sense of life; as a framework to validate what we know to be true deep within us yet cannot quite articulate. Remember the Walking Dead analogy from chapter four? The forgotten soul is trying to find its way out of the box, and the silly human points it to yet another empty box.

Religion is the design of humanity to give us some kind of purpose, some kind of method to the madness, so to speak, some kind of connection to the soul - because we inherently crave that connection. Organized religion offers us comfort, knowing that if we acknowledge a higher power, our existence makes a little more sense.

Unknowingly, we are freely exchanging our internal compass, our power, and our own soul's Source connection, for yet another box - an external source of guidance that is spoon-fed to us "for our safety" because it is too dangerous for us to go it alone. This is called religion, primarily Western religion, and if we make good choices within the confines of our religion, we will be rewarded for being obedient in the end—a dichotomy to the severest degree.

Discounting your hard-wired eternal soul's guidance as inferior and internalizing a man-made institution that is based upon the concept of "be good or pay the price at the end" and most absurdly, "you are too ignorant to figure it out for yourself, so we will tell you what God says" is a ludicrous concept. If we do good out of fear of punishment, are we really doing good?

Religious dogmatism steals the most important aspect of the soul's journey - personal accountability for your own growth, and sets you up for failure upon death, which is the ultimate goal, and the ultimate reason for life. The elevation of your soul's knowledge through active participation in your soul's journey... to do what you need to do in this human experience, to ascend (transform) into the next journey of your ancient self upon death is the objective.

You may be shocked to hear this, but death is the purpose of life. Contradictory, of course, but let me explain: The mission is to connect the body with the soul so you can live a beautiful life during this human experience, and upon actual death, you can ascend to the next journey of your soul, whatever that may be for you.

The win of life is to unbox your soul and merge it with your consciousness so you can do what you came here to do, learn what you came to learn, help who you came to help, and be stronger and better equipped on the other side to continue into your soul's eternal journey. This is soul ascension, and it is the only reason that you are alive. Thus, life is to be lived to prepare for your death, because death is just the beginning of your continuous soul journey; and for whatever reason is your purpose, what we do here matters to the next leg of our eternal journey.

To win at the Game of Life is to transition into death in the highest stage of soul understanding that you can get to in your short time in the physical body. This is the only objective and a challenge that you accepted when you agreed to be born. Imagine the surprise when your consciousness transitions into Source energy (your soul is your connection to Source) when the flesh finally wears out, only to realize that you wasted the entire experience living inside a box, serving the enemy, strengthening the very machine that consumed you.

You were supposed to help humanity, one by one, escape from the box - but you were instead seduced by the box itself. Consumed by the ease and comfort it provided, you betrayed yourself. This earthly realm is a battlefield, and the battle is to find your way out of that box.

Chapter 6

What Happens When You Die?

It's Not What You May Think It Is...

Regardless of your religion, your belief system, or your traditions, this is the question that we all want to know, and the driving force of many belief systems. What is really "out there"? What really happens after we take our very last breath? Despite the many and various teachings, when one is actually dying the blaring question remains to the end... What is really on the other side of all this? The fact remains that we really don't know. Despite all the rhetoric, no one really knows, 100% for sure what happens after death.

Some say you transfer to either heaven or hell upon a final judgment of your human actions to spend eternity in either reward or punishment. Some say you reincarnate just to do it all again and again with no real ending, while others say you continue to reincarnate until you get it right, yet others say you can choose to reincarnate or not.

Some believe we return to our home planet. Some say that when the physical body ends, there is nothing else. Others say that we transition into eternal bliss in a place called heaven, where souls are stockpiled in perpetual happiness as a reward for our experience. In addition to many other beliefs, everyone has some idea of what happens, but the only absolute truth is that no one knows.

We all spend our lives, in one way or another, avoiding death or preparing for death. In the beginning years, we hardly give it a thought, in the middle years we try to fight it off, in the end years we try to come to terms with it - but as the timeline of life ticks onward, the inevitable ending of our flesh, known as death, becomes very real and present. Oftentimes this change of focus from living to inevitable death happens when we witness the death of someone else, as the death transformation of someone else can be a catalyst of our transformation. Sometimes the purpose of one's death is to transform someone else.

Likewise, the birth of a child can trigger the pontification of your mortality. It's no coincidence that birth and death can affect us in the same way, because they are, fundamentally, the same process... one soul enters and another leaves... forcing the contemplation of your existence.

Many people are unnecessarily confused and afraid of death. If we could only understand the beauty of the transition and stop processing death from such a simplistic ego-based perspective, maybe we would live our experience here much differently. Instead of self-centric mourning, we should be rejoicing and wishing a hardy Bon Voyage instead. If only we could see the linear perspective of our eternal selves and understand that this is just a temporary exercise in soul ascension. It seems that, perhaps, on the other side of all this, it may be that the things that we obsess about now do not matter at all; but the boxed-in perspective of the limited human understanding confined to a measly 100 years of meaningless ego experiences prevails.

This life is so much more than what we think it is, and it has purpose and meaning to our eternal souls. Live like you are going to die, make every minute, and every experience count, and die with glory and honor that you will continue on eternally. Do not be afraid of death. Death is simply the transition of your eternal self back to your root source, the continued expression of your energetic force.

With the contemplation of death (or birth), many of us begin to wonder "What is the point, the purpose, of this life I am living?" It is at this marker that many begin to awaken to an inner stirring of their purpose. This leads to an exploration of the meaning of life.

Chapter 7

What Is the Meaning of Life?

W hat does it even mean to be alive? It is interesting to understand that what one believes about death lends itself to what one believes about life. Some say there is no purpose, that it is all just a biological process, and they only have one chance to live whatever represents a fulfilling life to them.

Others say we are here to acknowledge and worship a deity that will decide our fate according to the rules and regulations of written (and then rewritten) ancient books of protocol that should dictate our behaviors, and the following of these rules and regulations ensures a reward in the end. Some believe the kindness (or not) of our life actions will be repaid upon death, so they live to ensure this reciprocation. Still, others say that you will have repeated opportunities to re-do what you could not accomplish this time around. Some say this is hell, and we are here to redeem ourselves.

There are endless belief systems that dictate how we live this thing called life, but the question remains of why. Why are we here, and what is the point of all of it? What are we supposed to be doing and why?

If how we live is dictated by what we believe is on the other side of all this, then the logical deduction is that whatever is on the other side of this is IMPORTANT. It is important because the obvious conclusion is that the soul carries on. The essence of YOU is held in your soul. YOU will carry on eternally. In the meantime, you play a very important role in the fabric of humanity. Your soul shares with all others souls the foundational threads that bind us all together.

It is this aspect of your consciousness that is in touch with all the things that we share as human beings. We all crave intellectual expression, emotional connectedness, physical comfort, and inspiration. Having all of this brings a sense of peace to the human being.

The internal, unwavering desire for PEACE is the common thread between us. The definition of peace is "wholeness, tranquility, harmony" and it is what we all crave to create in our lives. Peace in the mind, peace in the emotions, peace in the satisfaction of life, peace in our sense of well-being. This is what all humans strive to achieve in this life, it's what we all do all day, every day... try to create internal equilibrium... but something is always missing.

To strive to create a sense of "wholeness" insinuates that something is missing. If we are trying to create peace in our lives, it must be missing, because, if we had it, we wouldn't be trying to find it. The missing piece of the puzzle is your recognition of, and connection to, your soul, which is an energetic extension of SOURCE, which vibes on a frequency of pure peace. The frequency of it at its core is peace.

You feel your soul, you return to your soul in sleep, you hear your soul speaking to you through your intuition, but most simply ignore it, and search endlessly for the peace that is already there. In our simplistic human understanding, disconnected from our soul, we try and try to create a sense of peace through our human understanding of how to do this - the only way you were ever allowed to know it - through distractions, addictions, and carnal pursuits. Feeding the wants and needs of the flesh, being filled for a moment then empty again. The opposing forces offer you everything to placate your desire for meaning to keep you disillusioned and impotent, and just weak enough to not fight against it, but fed enough to keep generating the low vibrational despair it feeds off.

We give all our valuable time in this very short lifetime in exchange for tangible resources so we can have the feeling of peace. Happiness is gained through success and achievement to acquire the things that are supposed to bring us peace... money, success, comfort, love... yet never really attaining peace because of the perpetual cycle of consumption and attainment. Constantly putting out effort and energy to maintain a sense of peace is inherently unpeaceful - an oxymoron in its most classic definition.

A perpetual cycle of savage hunting and consumption but never being fully satisfied because of the anticipation of the need for more, year after year until the release of death. The soul's separation from your daily reality causes this vicious cycle. Finding your soul, your true authentic self, and returning to it stops this cycle and allows you to be filled with peace, contentment, and satiety - clearing the way for your mission to emerge. Acknowledging your soul, merging it with your consciousness, and overriding the ego allows the purposeful path of your life to unfold.

Chapter 8

There Is Purpose: YOU Have Purpose

You were not born into the flesh simply abandoned to scratch and claw for your existence. You have been equipped with all the tools you need to live a peaceful, purposeful, and successful life. It all resides within you. Your ancient soul lives within you, and it (you) knows the way of your best and highest good, and if you will listen to it (yourself) it will show you the way of your journey and reveal to you the purpose of your life - your own personal path to peace.

It is your free will that will dictate how easy or hard the journey will be. Your flesh will either heed the direction of your soul, or it will ignore it. Those consumed by their egos (human nature and survival instincts) are blinded and will ignore it, as they cannot understand anything greater than their own human experience. Those who choose to listen and follow will be enlightened to a better way, an easier way, a peaceful way of maneuvering and existing in the human experience. Free will dictates both.

Free will is the gift to all humanity, as true Source energy will not ever force you to align with it. You are free to choose how you live your life. You are not a slave to an all-knowing supreme being. You are an important piece of an ancient eternal concept, threads in the tapestry of an infinite universe, and you have the freedom to willingly engage with universal order, or not. Your free will decides your destiny at the death transition, because free will decides how you live, and how you live in your physical experience will dictate the next leg of your soul's journey, your eternal journey.

Soul ascension is the ultimate objective. Soul ascension is not about living a moral life out of fear of punishment, it's not about how many good things you do while you are alive, it's not about anything but your free will to surrender to your soul's guidance, in turn, fulfilling your purposeful existence in this human experience. Your soul's guidance IS your morality, it IS the good inside you.

Being in touch with the all-consuming peace of your soul's journey negates the need for an overarching concept of institutional beliefs. Beliefs that are designed to keep you accountable while stealing your own personal accountability for your free will choices through promises of forgiveness, or a guarantee of reward in the afterlife, or the disillusionment that you have control over the quality of your experience with education or money.

Your "reward" for living this life is ascension into the next leg of the journey. With soul accountability comes all the natural outputs of being at peace internally. Love, kindness, serenity, acceptance, and tranquility will become your coping mechanisms, and a deep knowing of purpose then oozes into your daily life, and onto those around you... these are the things a soulful being organically produces, and these are the things that the human ego strives to duplicate in the absence of soulful purpose.

What IS your SOUL and where does it come from? That is the million- dollar question. According to Wikipedia, "In many religious and philosophical traditions, the soul is the spiritual essence of a person, which includes one's identity, personality, and memories - an immaterial aspect or essence of a living being that is believed to be able to survive physical death.".

Many people believe many things about where the soul comes from, but for this book, we will simply accept that it just is, and we will accept whatever origin you choose to believe in, because how it was formed is irrelevant to this discussion. Your relationship with it is our only concern. For this book, Source is the origin of your soul, whatever label you feel comfortable addressing it as is fine by me.

The mission is to acknowledge the missing link, seek it out, incorporate it into your consciousness, live through it, and in the end, experience joyous soul ascension through death. The objective of this game called life is for you to overcome your flesh and find your soul, to find your true self, to embrace and honor who you truly are - the soul that IS the threads that you are sewn from. There is purpose and meaning to your existence.

Chapter 9

How To Find Your Soul Under the Layers of Your Skin

The common thread of all humanity stems from Source energy. Your soul is directly rooted in Source energy (Source > Soul > Human), and therefore interconnected to all living things. Source energy IS a pure frequency of an all-knowing sense of peace which equates to the purest form of love. There is almost no other way to describe this energy. Being connected to your soul is being connected to Source, and being connected to Source brings an all-consuming peace.

Acknowledging and accepting that your soul speaks to your consciousness through your intuition, and actively, kinetically, following the guidance of your soul through your intuition, reinforced by signs and synchronicities around you, and accepting what it is telling you, even when you want to argue with it, is the honoring of your ancient self and the wisdom that it holds.

By knowing that you know all is well in every aspect of your life, even in the face of challenges, you are surrendering to your soul path instead of your flesh path. You will be led on the course of life that is in your best and highest good, always, every time, even when you don't completely understand why. This active surrender leads to soul ascension, as only in this understanding can Source lead you and guide you in the direction that you need to go, to do what you came here to do, for the best and highest good of yourself, those around you, and your purpose... your own personal soul mission.

What IS your purpose, you ask? Soul Ascension. That is your only purpose in this lifetime. That's it, that's all... soul ascension. Nothing else.

Understanding this relieves you of all the pressure that is involved in trying to make your way in this game we call life. Imagine the peace you will have   if you are allowed to simply stop TRYING to create a good life and step into the life you were always meant to live. This is easy to do when you stop trying to control the outcome. Letting go of control is the hard part. To let go of control, you must surrender your presumptuous all-knowing ego to an intangible life force.

For many people, this is not an easy thing to do because our identity has been formed and fed for all our lives to accept the human experience as the only reality, and the soul experience as something too difficult for you to understand on your own. Control is leverage, and believe me, you have no leverage when it comes to the universal order of things.

We are taught by the system of humanity to work hard, get stuff, pay the system, and seek our spiritual needs from an institution that says you are not able to understand your soul except through the explanation and teachings of humans who are called to a higher spiritual purpose than you. This is all the big show, the big lie, that keeps you from soul ascension.

You see, as much as there is pure Source energy, physics says there is also, and always will be, an opposing vibrational energy source (yin/yang, good/evil, light/dark, masculine/feminine, positive/negative) that would love nothing more than to see you live and die in the shallows of your human experience, keeping enlightenment from you through your ignorance of your true power - the power of knowing your own soul, the power of connection to Source.

If you break free from the confines of this world through awakening and enlightenment, you now become a threat to the system that is designed to suppress your connection to Source so it can consume your life force as a resource to keep the machine's momentum - a soul-sucking vacuum of mechanical living that wants to thwart your soul ascension, steal your power, and deliver you to death defeated.

Why else would the world we live in be consumed by idolatry? Falling at the feet of the god of comfort and worshiping your existence through the constant consumption of ego validation in all of its various forms, with an enormous ignorance of your true purpose. This is the extent of existence for many, many people. Most will live and die in this box.

The process of Ascension is the raising of your frequency to a higher vibration (explained further in the following chapters), shedding and controlling your ego, and shifting into an elevated level of consciousness (also explained in the next chapters). THIS IS the point of being alive, this IS the challenge that you are to conquer, and this IS the key to living a peaceful and mindful life. This IS the end game.

Awakening through enlightenment, enlightenment through questioning, questioning through awakening from the sedation of the opposing forces that need you to be in perpetual slumber. All so you do not become a threat to the enslavement that works so well for the human system (opposing forces), and quite frankly the theft of your true purpose. Wake up and see the world around you with new eyes, through the vision of your eternal soul instead of your simple flesh. This human experience is the battleground for your soul to find its way. We all came here to learn to conquer THE EGO. If you can conquer the ego (human nature), you win. That's the game we are all playing here.

The ego represents your basic, mechanical human understanding of life. The box. From the moment you took your first breath in this meat suit, you have been subject to the ego, the coping mechanism by which to survive. I want what I want, and I'm going to do whatever it is that I must do to get it. As simple as a snack from the fridge to world domination, this same drive is human nature.

The objective, remember, is ASCENSION, and conquering our ego is conquering our flesh, which is the key to ascension.

Chapter 10

The Ancient Secrets:

What You May Not Know

So how do you conquer the ego and ascend? Well, I'm about to tell you how to do this in the following chapters. I'm going to explain to you the ultimate guide to living a successful life through spiritual growth and purpose, ultimately to ascend in the next adventure of your soul's journey. These spiritual "secrets" are revealed in the layers of awakening and gauged according to your depth of understanding.

Why is such an important concept a "secret"? Simply because when you are asleep, you cannot understand, you are blind; and to those who begin to awaken from the human slumber, the secrets are revealed. The concept of ascension is lost in the boxed-in blindness.

Think of your awakening as your mind being locked in a box (the box that has been referenced throughout this book). Layer after layer, box inside a box, inside yet another box. The big box is what you are born into, the smaller boxes inside the big box contain your identity and your beliefs. To break free from the inner boxes, you must begin to think outside the box.

When you begin to question your belief system, you will begin to question your identity. When you begin to question your identity, you will begin to question your belief system. When you question your identity in relation to your beliefs, and vice versa, you begin to question your entire life. The person who questions their fundamental beliefs is catapulted into the first concept of soul understanding to spend as much time as it takes to get out of the next box, your identity - and so forth and so on until you finally break free from the final box of ego death - arriving at true soul connection catapulting you into soul ascension.

During my observation of life, my own personal experiences, in my profession as a healer via psychospiritual channeling (I act as a medium to channel your soul's messages that are blocked my your human mind in order to set you free - I am a "seed planter"), in the lives of my clients and family, my studies, and most importantly according to the universal laws of spiritual growth where one understanding cannot happen without the other - I have surmised that there are 21 fundamental phases of spiritual evolution.

The first time around, upon initial awakening, the concepts unfold in order and then overlap. One building upon the other to ensure time for digestion. As we experience awakening and soul growth they begin interlacing through the course of our lives, endlessly building upon each other through the course of our human existence, and perhaps beyond.

21 concepts may seem overwhelming... but for some this unveiling will happen at lightning speed, and for others it will be at a snail's pace, it just depends upon how much you desire to engage with it, and how much of your ancient soul has already conquered in your previous journeys. Some of it will feel like the clicking of puzzle pieces in your life, and some of it will be filled with challenges. Such is the journey of your awakening, and your progression lies entirely upon your free will, at your chosen pace.

As we learn the lessons associated with each concept and layer, that piece of our inner being levels up in the concept of ascension, with the ultimate goal being to gain as much as you can from this experience by uniting your soul with your consciousness. Just like any education, you are entering into your spiritual education at ground zero, how you progress depends on your motivation.

These 21 concepts are all the processes of ego death. Ego death is the objective, soul ascension is the goal. Ego control is ego death. Your ego, your human nature will never die as it is the human frontman, but learning to control your ego takes its power away.

And allows you to conquer your flesh nature so you can live in your soul nature and ASCEND in your soul's next journey upon the inevitable death transition. The following exploration of the concepts and layers of spiritual transformation will walk you through what's happening as you awaken from your long slumber and show you how to navigate it successfully.

The following chapter, Chapter 11 is huge, not only in length but in subject matter as well. It is very important and the bedrock of your growth. You will reference this chapter continuously as you grow and learn. It is followed by 6 more chapters containing the 21 concepts. Most concepts have several steps to the process. Each concept leads to the next, and one cannot be digested without the other. They are symbiotic in nature - the action of one leads to the action of the next. They are meant to provoke thought, contemplation, and movement - they are not a checklist of things to do.

So, slow down, take your time, and just simply feel what these concepts bring to your attention. Check your silly humanness at the door, along with your ego and your expectations. Open your mind and unbox your soul.

Chapter 11

Your Internal Life:

3 Concepts That Will

Transform Your Journey

CONCEPT 1: GROUND ZERO (YOUR MIND)

Zero represents nothingness because here is where you will empty your mind. One is the number of new beginnings, new opportunities, new everything, and 11 is a soul path number. Chapter 11, Concept 1, ground zero is where you will begin. The following concepts are the absolute most important cornerstones that you need to know to create a meaningful and peaceful life.

It is at this level you will begin to build a new life on new ground with a new foundation. This concept is the absolute bedrock of your life, and you cannot possibly fully grow until the layers of this concept are understood, according to your own personal soul path.

These are the most important lessons to learn in all of your human existence. You will return to this concept over and over again to refine your growth.

Let's begin...

C onceptualize your mind as a brand-new plot of raw land, valuable land that you're going to develop as the foundation for your life, to grow and flourish and live in peaceful harmony. A place that you knew was out there somewhere, the place you've been searching for, but never seem to find, or at least not for very long.

Within the box of your life, you have climbed over seemingly insurmountable mountains and crossed treacherous rivers, traveled far and wide searching for this peaceful place. The journey thus far has been strenuous and difficult, weighted with anxiety and emptiness, strapped with stress and fear. Then, a small glimmering of something through the cracks in the box catches your attention, and you don't know why, but you are compelled to investigate, and when you do, you only see more and more that you want to explore outside the box.

Here is where you become awakened... and now, after a heavy journey all on your own, you have arrived at the threshold of a complete transformation, a spiritual awakening by which the old you will shed away and the new you will flourish... and it's been at your feet all this time. This piece of land is the foundation that you will build your new, unboxed life upon, develop your internal desire for something better, and cooperate with your soul's knowing that there is something better than the box that you are living in.

Step One: Taking Inventory

When you finally arrive at your new piece of land, you will stand on the highest point and take in all that you have to work with. The first thing you are going to do is assess the situation:

What do you see, what do you smell, and what are your hopes and dreams to build here? What inspires you to build here? Inspiration is the soul's guidance that you are headed in the right direction. What do you want your life to be like? Think about it, envision it, down to the smallest details. Write a short, detailed story about what your future looks like in the space below.

_____

_____

_____

_____

_____

_____

_____

_____

_____

_____

_____

_____

Now, let's think about how you're going to grow this piece of land into the place where you will live your life:

What is in the way? You can't build on land that is consumed by overgrowth, so what kind of debris needs to be removed? Vines, rocks, trash, old fencing, holes to be filled, land to be leveled? What are your obstacles to clearing the real estate of your mind? Are there boulders that need to be dug up and removed, or stumbling blocks to the smooth foundation required to build your future?

Let's assess the foundation of your mind... childhood woundings, mommy issues, daddy issues? We all have them because no human is perfect, and our parents are humans, and no matter how great your childhood was, no one escapes childhood unscathed; and every single one of our adult issues can be traced back to your childhood, mom, and dad. Dig it up, research it (abandonment issues, narcissistic parent, abuse, submissive parent, absent parents, imposter syndrome, PTSD, etc. - choose your poison), make sense of it (but don't obsess about it - it is what it is), and haul it away.

In reality, none of it was really about you... it was/is always about them, always about them. Any other soul born to these people under any other name at the time you were born would have the same experiences that you had. We are all just collateral damage in the lives of ego-driven humans. It was not personal, it was not about you, so stop internalizing it, and stop taking it all so personally. If you turned on the water faucet and sludge came out, would you blame yourself?

No. It's the city water system's or the well diggers' fault. Same thing for you - it wasn't your fault that you were collateral damage in the lives of people who were not in control of themselves, for whatever reason (usually repeated family cycles), consumed by their simplistic flesh experience. They just spewed their unhealed wounds onto you, and you, as a child, internalized this as your identity.

Fallen branches, or thorn bushes? Toxic relationships that are rooted and recycled repeatedly in unaddressed childhood wounds, internalized mistreatment, and a deep-rooted self-narrative that are not your own words? Cut it down and burn it. Let the ashes blow away in the wind and let the smoldering coals finally bring an end to something that was, ultimately, not even about you.

Poison ivy, itchy weeds, biting ants, a hornet's nest maybe? What are your triggers? Growth means emotional maturity, and emotional maturity means being in control of your emotions. Your triggers are your responsibility to identify and control. Are you bitter and angry, or sad and depressed? Why - because you got the short end of the stick, the bad hand of cards, a raw deal in life? Welcome to the Club. Everyone has some kind of story, and yours may be really bad, but you have a choice in how you process your life experiences. You can let your past eat you alive like a disease (and it will) or you can take a step back, reassess your perspective, and use everything as inspiration for the rest of your life.

Use what was supposed to break you as fuel for your success. Read this book to the end and then reevaluate what you are manifesting in your life. Document in the space below what psychological issues you are internalizing to be your truth based upon someone else's inability to handle their own demons, their own brokenness. What is in the trash bag that they have handed to you? Low self-esteem? Anger? Abandonment? Emotional rejection? Fear? Narcissism? Let it all go in the space below.

_____

_____

_____

_____

_____

_____

_____

_____

_____

_____

_____

_____

_____

_____

_____

_____

_____

Step Two: What Are Your Assets?

After the overgrowth and obstacles are addressed, step two is to identify your assets: Is there a creek, or a river, or a well for water? Find the good in yourself and your life. Speak well of yourself and be kind to your inner child.

How about honeysuckle trees, berry bushes, or fruit trees? What kind of fruit do you want to bear in your life? Does your countenance shine like sunshine and is your frequency attracting the bees that will pollinate your dreams, or are you still dealing with the hornet's nest?

See the beauty of yourself, see the importance of the contribution that you bring to your life through the threads of your ancient self. You are important, you are needed, and you can make a difference. Despite what you may believe about yourself, you are important, your existence has meaning, and you have purpose. What have the hardships of your life taught you? How can you help others through similar struggles? What kind of kindness and compassion have you collected within yourself?

What is your strength? Take a minute to note the beautiful threads that make up who you are at the core:

_____

_____

_____

_____

_____

_____

_____

_____

Now that we've cleaned things up a bit, let's see what kind of foundation we've got to work with. A solid foundation, clear of debris is fundamental for structural success. Is your ground overrun with crusty old stalks of things that once were alive, but now are just simply in the way of new growth? Are the people you surround yourself with helping or hindering your awakening? Are they stumbling blocks or stepping stones?

Fruit-bearing trees or thorny vines? If the situations, circumstances, and people in your life are not helping you, they are hindering you. Any situation or relationship that takes hard work to maintain isn't a peaceful relationship, so why would you? This is not to say that you should abandon anyone or anything because the situation needs effort, but if your effort is consistently creating discourse in your daily life, you must reconsider why you are choosing to make it work – what wound is it feeding inside of you? Why does your wounded inner child need that particular relationship?

Remember the linear soul perspective? Your relationships with people, places, and things who are incapable of keeping in step with your spiritual growth will mean nothing, zero, nothing on the other side of this experience. These relationships are a waste of your precious time, they consume the energy that you need to grow. Soulful people have soulful relationships. Peaceful relationships. Like attracts like, so be careful who you like.

Holding space with flesh-driven people is a waste of time. Cut it all down so you can see the soil and get back to the true foundation of who you are... the beautiful soul that is meant to live a peaceful life.

Take a moment to reflect on the upsetting relationships in your life. Analyze why you remain engaged (genetics are not enough). You cannot heal someone who doesn't desire to heal. The ONLY way someone changes is when they get sick and tired of their own BS. That's why you are reading this book, because you crave the change that your awakening is making you aware of. If one does not see their own shortcomings, there is absolutely nothing you can do to help them - not friends, not family, not your children, not your spouse.

In the space below, reflect upon why you are in the unsatisfying relationships that you cling to?

_____
_____
_____
_____
_____
_____
_____
_____
_____
_____
_____

Step Three: Prepping The Ground

Once the land is cleared, and the foundation is prepped, we need to fertilize with components that will procure good growth. Begin with re-writing your self-narrative - the internal belief system that was formed when you were in the box. Now that you've cleared some real estate in your mind, who are you compared to who you want to be and how did you get here?

What do you hear in your head? The self-talk you have in your head is either the wounded child or the healed adult. What are you saying to yourself? Is the wounded child still running your emotional life, or are you now looking out for yourself from a healed adult perspective?

Are you guarding that wounded child, looking out for him/her/them, making choices that are good for it? Have you set it free to be happy so you can be free? Go inside and explain to the inner child what you have healed as an adult - that it was never personal against you, but that your people were just unhealed too. They hurt you because they were consumed with themselves, consumed with their own pain, too weak to break out of the box - not because you deserved it. This internal narrative will be the nutrients to the seeds that you will sow in your life, so be careful what you believe about yourself.

What do you believe about yourself?

What do you want to believe about yourself?

Finally, we will sprinkle forgiveness all over the soil - forgiveness of our ignorance, and the ignorance of others - because before we desire to awaken, we are all just simply, numbly, asleep. You cannot be held accountable for that which you did not know, and the people who put you in the box are just as consumed with their self-centric egos as you were. They stole your power in their never-ending quest to be powerful in their own mind. Misguided, misaligned, and missing the integral components of their soul.

I say "were" because if you made it this far, you are interested in learning a better way to be. Any wrongdoing perpetrated by anyone, even you, is never about the person on the receiving end, it's about the person themselves. We should never take anything personally because everyone is always projecting their internal workings outward, and if they are unhealed, they will spew chaos onto everyone. Any other person in the same place at the same time would get the same. It's not about you, it's about them.

So stop internalizing once and for all - and let it go so you do not continue to grow briars and thorns. We want the foundation to be healthy and fertile!

Who and what do you need to let go of?

_____

_____

_____

_____

_____

_____

_____

_____

_____

_____

_____

_____

_____

_____

_____

_____

_____

_____

Step Four: Planting The Seeds

Understand that your mind is the absolute most powerful tool that you have been given.

It is the seedbed of all creation, and it most certainly creates your reality, whether you like it or not. What ruminates in your subconscious mind becomes your reality. Period. End of story. Your deep internal self-talk creates your reality based upon the "voices" in your mind, your internal self-narrative.

What you generate in your mind is your reality. Change the self- narrative and you will change your reality. The power of manifestation is a golden gift of your eternal soul and the absolute most important tool to creating the life YOU want to live. Don't squander it by accepting an identity that you did not choose to create. Be who you WANT to be instead of being what you have been told that you are.

Handle your internal business by diving into the box that you have been living in and sorting through the childhood conditioning (good, bad, or otherwise) that has gotten you to where you are right now, because those seeds have grown inside of you, and they dictate the fruit that you bear in your life.

Let go of your human labels, and restructure your expectations of yourself, the expectations of family, society, education, and religion. Free yourself from the prison of your mind and embrace and utilize the power of your thought-life to create a seedbed that has the fertility to grow who you truly ARE - a soul having a human experience, not a human having a soul experience.

Stop casting the seeds of your life on the barren ground - ground that is so overgrown with the weathered stalks of the expectations of everyone and everything that has ever had access to your subconscious mind. There is no room to grow a new internal narrative until you pull some weeds. Till up the soil of your mind, plant new seeds of growth, and begin to create a clean and clear plot of real estate by which to build upon, to become something more than you are now.

Begin to internalize and understand the linear concept of being alive vs the human boxed-in timeline: eternal soul > body/life > eternal soul. Begin to see this life as a mission of growth, as an act of transformation that has significance to the next leg of your soul's journey, YOUR journey through eternity.

When you begin to understand that this life is not the beginning or the end, but merely an opportunity to ascend, the people, places, things, and experiences that you have will mean something more significant to you. The silly things that we obsess about become meaningless. The silly relationships that consume our internal and external space become irrelevant. The desires of the flesh become simple stupidity, and the whole of everything is revealed to you in increments that are digestible in your consciousness.

Reach deeply into yourself and ask your ancient self, your soul... who am I, what is my purpose, and how do I accomplish it? Then, listen to it. Follow the guidance that it gives you and act in that direction. Sow these seeds into the fresh new ground that you have worked so hard to create.

This is The Awakening. The mind is the gateway to all things.

CONCEPT 2: FOLLOWING THE VOICE WITHIN

This concept begins in the previous understanding of emptying the box in your subconscious mind, which allows your intuition to be heard in your consciousness. Once you understand and acknowledge soul connection, you become more aware of the communication. It will take some practice because you are so used to the frantic, belligerent ego barking instructions at you, that the soft whispering of Source is sometimes missed.

Step One: Finding Your True North

Be attentive and follow your inner knowings with intention and purpose, it is your True North. It comes from the chest, not from the head. You will feel your intuition, you will hear your mind. Pointing your mind toward your intuition is always, every time, going to lead you to the path of your best and highest good in this physical experience, whether you understand it or not, whether you agree with it or not. Find the voice of your soul and think in that direction. In your daily decisions, ask yourself "what is my soul saying?" and do it without question.

Step Two: Letting Go of Control

Let go of control. Have faith that the Source of everything knows better than you. It is your internal compass, and part of the tools that we are all equipped with to live an amazing life. The struggle for every human being on this planet is the same, no matter the situation or circumstances... the struggle between that which you know to be true and, that which you do not want to accept as the truth. Stop overriding your intuition with your ego's misguided infinite wisdom. Stop trying to control things. Find peace in the journey even when you don't understand (just yet) or agree. Trust your intuition, your ancient soul will never steer you wrong.

As stated before, these layers intertwine with one another, and if you have not cleared the ground from the previous layers, you will have limited ability to conceptualize this layer, as the ground is not yet ready to grow a new understanding, and you will find yourself fighting against it. Do the work at Ground Zero so you can succeed here.

CONCEPT 3: THE INTEGRATION

Tilling up the soil, searching for your True North, and letting go of control facilitates the integration of your mind with your soul. You are literally performing alchemy in your life by joining your consciousness with your subconsciousness. Taking two separate energies and combining them into one to create something that didn't exist before. Alchemy.

Knowing that your thoughts create your reality, and your intuition is your guidance system, it just makes logical sense that if you focus your thought life on your intuition , you'll always end up in the best possible position. Make the connection of your soul to your flesh a collaboration between your human experience and your soul's mission.

Step One: What Feels Right IS Right

What do your guts say? Surrender to your intuition and point your thought life towards it to kinetically participate in the path of your best and highest good. Perfecting this takes practice and patience, but the more you try to do this, the more natural it becomes.

Step Two: The Knowing

Create an internal life of peace and serenity by knowing that you know all is well in the eternal order of the universe. Know that you are being guided and led to the meaning of YOUR life by the very soul that IS you. This is where you learn to stop doubting your connection to Source through your soul and create in your internal world a symbiotic balance between the human you and the eternal you. This is where the linear, unending timeline begins to take precedence over the box mentality.

Step Three: Recognizing Your Ego

This can be a challenge because many only know the voice of the ego. Differentiate between the voice of your ego and the prompting of your soul. Recognize when the ego wants what it wants and weigh it against your new-found soul. Live by your soul's understanding. Every day, all day, in everything. Ask and you will be shown, seek and you will find, go and you will be guided. Consistently ask, and consistently follow, and you will consistently find peace in all that you do. Point your mind to your intuition and execute accordingly. Turn the tables on yourself and begin to override the ego with intuitive understanding instead of overriding the soul with human understanding.

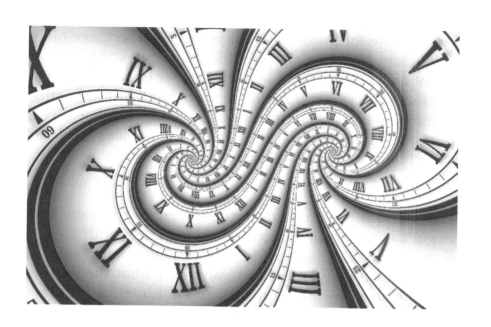

Chapter 12

Your External Life: How to Live Your Truth

CONCEPT 4: THE EXECUTION

A t this level, you will either step forward in your growth or go back into concept one to acquire more understanding, and that is perfectly ok. Remember, this is all on your timeline, according to your desire for growth. When you get to the place of consistency in your thought life by manifesting your intuition, the next step is to execute it in your reality. At this time, you will no longer care that you are living differently than everyone else, you will no longer care that others don't understand your life choices, and you will no longer desire to be a part of the flock.

You will want to step out of the internal processes and begin to build your outside world to reflect your internal world (chapter 11). You will confidently let your freak flag fly, not caring anymore about marching to the beat of your own drum, and confidently embrace this new way of life. You will now step out of the box and into a linear perspective of your existence by creating your physical life to reflect your newfound understandings.

Step 1: Changing Perspectives

This is where we differentiate between the material aspect of life and the spiritual aspect of life. We begin to desire to create our real life into a duplication of our spiritual life. Don't be surprised when you begin to desire a career change, a relationship change, or an environmental change. What meant something to your life before may shift and change at this time. You will feel the aliveness of everything, and bounce with a different step.

Step 2: Brick by Brick

You will begin to seek out like-minded people, teachers, and information. Fill your mind with new knowledge, new concepts, and a positive self-narrative. This is where you begin to level up. Brick by brick, constructing the external framework based on the growing internal overflow. This is where your seeds begin to take root and sprout with a new identity, a new life.

CONCEPT 5: THE FOUNDATION

B eliefs. Values. Morality. Structure. This is where you completely break free. This lesson is where you will be asked by your soul to plant the foundation stones by which you will now stand, in a belief system that dictates everything you do from now on. What side of the fence is your faith planted on? You can't have one foot on each side - one in the ego, one in the soul. The world will tell you that you can, but I assure you that is a lie. Your soul path is either all in or all out. The Universe can only divinely orchestrate the steps of your path if are participating of your own free will.

Remember the concept of free will? If your free will follows your soul's path, then the Universe can make things happen. The threads of the tapestry are connected. When you decide to do it your way instead, the Universe has no choice but to stand back and wait for you to get back on track. If you veer off on your own by denying your intuitive guidance, you veer from the path of your best and highest good according to the tapestry of Universal Order. So, it waits, sometimes an eternity, for you to come home. Rest assured, it is always there when your free will reaches out, but in the meantime, on your own, you are on your own. So, are you all in, or are you out?

Step 1: Who Are You vs. Who You Want to Be

What do you believe about life, your existence? Who are you? What are your expectations of life? What are you truly committed to? This is where you create your own identity, stop accepting what you are supposed to be, and begin BEING who you are created to be. This is where the previous concepts are solidified in your consciousness, creating a new belief system, a new foundation by which to stand in your newfound strength.

Step 2: Unpacking

Moving in and unpacking the boxes so-to-speak. Like moving from a home you've occupied for your entire life, going through each box, and wondering why you've even kept these things around all this time. You will be remodeling your life by unpacking your old belief systems and rebuilding, piece by piece. You will remain here until every box on the surface level is unpacked, sorted through, and put away. Just like moving houses, your procrastination to unpack will dictate how long you stay in this state.

CONCEPT 6: YOUR FREQUENCY

At this leg of the journey, you will begin to engage with others while standing upon your new belief system. As you come through the metamorphosis of all the previous layers, you will now begin to find your tribe. This lesson is about energetic attraction. Like attracts like, birds of a feather flock together.

Scientific fact: all energy has a frequency, and frequency has a vibration. This is perfectly exemplified by music. Music is a frequency that creates a vibration, and it can make you feel in many ways. You are energy, your aliveness is your energy. Your human body is the ideal composition to conduct electricity... water, salt, and tissue. Your brain fires off electrical impulses all day, every day. This energy is projected approximately 5 feet outward from your body (your aura). We all emit an energetic frequency and receive energy from everyone and everything. High-frequency energy attracts high-vibing energy, and low- frequency energy gravitates towards low vibrations. A high vibration pushes away a low vibration. A high frequency rises above a low frequency and attracts the same. You attract what you emit.

Step 1: Your Vibes

WHO are you attracting into your life? If you are still holding space with the same low-frequency people from your past, or continually attracting the same ol' type of person, you are not growing. Growth in your spirituality will organically displace those who are holding you back through your vibrations.

Like attracts like, so if you are vibing high, you will attract higher-frequency beings into your life, and the low- frequency people will be repelled by you, and you by them. This is a tell-tale sign of your progress. Look around your life... who is attracted to you? How are you vibing? And who are you vibing with?

Step 2: Uncomfortable Truth

If you are unwilling to grow beyond the low-vibrational people who are incapable of keeping step with you, if you are holding onto the identity that these people represent in your life, you will not go past this point, and you will need to revisit all of the previous concepts, over and over again to master this concept, and that's ok.

CONCEPT 7: EFFORT

Self-control. Will power. Determination. These attributes unwrap concepts that allow you to push forward in the journey. This is the place where you decide that you are prepared to move forward. This is where the Universe reciprocates your efforts, or more specifically, this is where YOUR energetic movement begins to vibe with the Universe. This is a movement forward. You have put in the effort to understand and internalize the previous layers.

You have exhibited the ability to recognize your mind as the soil of your life, gained control over your ego, poured in the willpower to change your foundational belief system from flesh-based to soul-based, you are in understanding of your frequency and vibration, and through self-exploration, reflection, and assessment, you have demonstrated determination to grow and learn.

Listen carefully to your intuition, point your mind in that direction, execute in the path that unfolds before you, stand upon a new internal structure, sort through those in your life who are holding back, and glide into the next phase of your life as a newly awakened little soul, and step into your new-found strength.

CONCEPT 8: STRENGTH

This lesson is akin to the caterpillar emerging as the butterfly after a long cocooning. When the caterpillar stitches itself inside the chrysalis, he doesn't understand why he is doing this, he just simply feels compelled to do it. This is representative of your previous inner knowing that something needs to change, and, being compelled internally, you sought out change through learning, healing, and understanding, through reconnection to your true self through your acknowledgment of your soul's calling... and now you find yourself here.

Step 1: Overcoming

Here is where you will have the strength to overcome instead of succumbing to the difficulties of being alive. The peeling away of what has always been, and the embracing of what is now. Emerging from the goo as a butterfly, seeing for the first time from a perspective that was hidden when you were crawling on the ground. A higher perspective is now a reality. In this understanding, you are now strong and courageous enough to fight the good fight. You will feel empowered and inspired, like a seedling stretching towards the sun. Things are clicking, and your life is changing.

Step 2: Changes

Many changes will occur in your life now. The old you is disappearing and the new you, the spiritual you, is emerging. The strength required to keep going will be found here, as you step into your power, proud of who you have become, and fearlessly unapologetic about your accomplishment.

Chapter 13

Learning to Communicate with the Source

CONCEPT 9: LEVELING UP

Now the new you will learn to initiate communication with Source instead of waiting for Source to communicate with you. Soul searching and introspection, contemplation and reflection from a new place, a place of Source connection.

Step 1: Listening

This is where you are humbled by your previous ignorance and begin to seek out Source intervention as opposed to just waiting for it. This is a time of deep introspection and soul searching where you intentionally crave to connect to Source energy, seeking out wisdom through actively asking and quietly listening. The training wheels are coming off. Your intuitive abilities are being exercised.

Now you will begin to understand that it's not just your higher self (soul) speaking to you, but true communion with Source (because your soul is rooted in Source energy), an exchange between the two of you articulated through the knowing in your intuition, and signs and synchronicities in the situations and circumstances around you.

You will become sensitive to your power. Soul searching, seeking answers, learning to ASK your intuition, and being able to perceive the answers. This sets you up for the next phase of your journey.

Step 2: Being Proactive

Instead of waiting for direction, you are proactively asking for direction. Get quiet. Be still. Calm your senses and ask to commune with Source. This is where you learn to disassociate with your flesh and step inside your subconscious mind, bringing your soul to the surface and joining forces with your comprehensive understanding that you are one with the universe and who you are is a very important part of the tapestry of the eternal universe. Meditation isn't only found in the cross-legged posture of "Om", it is found wherever you find the peace of silence. Practice being quiet, practice inviting Source into your consciousness.

CONCEPT 10: THE TURNING POINT

This is THE turning point in your awakening, as your free will wants nothing more than to be in alignment with Source. This "faith" that you have created by the application of all the previous lessons puts you in a position not only to receive the blessings of Source, but to recognize Source when it shows up. This is the "ah ha" moment that allows the divine orchestration of your path.

It is a turning point in your life, and it leads you to good fortune, and the activation of your ability to manifest your reality supernaturally. The exercising of the concepts on the way to this concept has been active growth, but this concept is THE turning point that clears the way for Universal Order to be laid out before you. Big life changes and new opportunities magically materialize in your life. Recognize the Universal Order unfolding in your life and act accordingly. Congratulations! You have worked so hard to get here. Roll with it and just let it happen!

Chapter 14

Learning to Maintain
Control of Yourself

CONCEPT 11: ACCOUNTABILITY

This understanding, like all the others before it,
feeds off of the previous concepts and layers.
Concepts 1-10 should be taking root and
growing. Now you have been through basic training
and spiritual boot camp. Because you have developed

the fundamental concepts required to progress into the remaining concepts, here is where you are now held accountable for your progression forward. Will you continue to surrender or, now that you have elevated your consciousness, will you take the reins back and mistakenly think that you have arrived? It is now up to you to seek out Source in all things and be in tune with your soul's path.

Step 1: What Do Your Guts Say?

Like the frequency vibrations discussed in concept six, at this point, you should be at a frequency level that can interpret literal guidance from Source - not just cognizant of your soul's existence, but truly communicating with Source. Thus a leveling up of your responsibility is required. What is in your best and highest good will always be shown to you, and you are now responsible for acting upon it, all the time, every time, without arguing.

Step 2: Are You Stuck on Repeat?

You are heavily accountable for your journey from this point forward. This step can be a sticking point for some because once one gets here, they seem to think that this is the level of attainment that they have been striving for. Once they see things coming together in their lives, they stop seeking and back-step into the ego, which sets you back into whatever concept(s) you need to redo. Be careful here. This is a slippery slope.

Remember, your newfound power has come from your soul's guidance, not your ego's guidance. Don't let the ol' meat suit weasel its way back in.

CONCEPT 12:

CONTEMPLATING YOUR MOTIVATIONS

I t is now time to reflect and assess upon what may be obstacles to your forward movement. Here, you will contemplate where you came from and where you are going, and surrender to the things that need to be let go once and for all... or not.

Step 1: Trimming The Ragged Edges

Take inventory of everything and let loose the remaining fragments of your old self. Reevaluate your motivations for not letting go, understand why you don't want to let go by revisiting and contemplating the previous concepts... and let them go so they don't trip you up along the rest of your journey. This is the scrubbing out of any residual necrosis in your life to prepare you even further for what is to come.

Step 2: Vision

The scrubbing that comes with this level of growth can be both soothing and harsh. This is a new vision of who you are, where you came from, and where you are going. The time is now to reevaluate your progress and reevaluate your vision of the future.

Chapter 15

The Transformation of Your Life

CONCEPT 13: THE DEATH OF YOU

Once again, due to ALL of the previous concepts and layers, and particularly because of the previous lesson, all things as they were will come to an end for you to step through the threshold of birth. The birth of an awakened you, a soulful you, a purposeful you. This is, of course, a metaphorical death. Death, as we know, is the absolute end of a conduit for our energetic expression. The former energetic expression of yourself created your previous existence. The new enlightened, awakened, elevated energetic expression of you is going to create your new reality. When the flesh dies, the soul ascends.

This is the beginning of the end - the final descent into ego death, the final separation of your rote human participation, and the birth of your truth. Your energetic expression is catapulting you to wisdom and growth. This is a pivotal transformation with immense forward momentum. You will find yourself lingering between two worlds for a while, fully present in the transformation, but looking back in a surreal, disconnectedness as you wave goodbye.

Step 1: Rebirth

Who you were in your humanness at the beginning of this journey should no longer exist. This is the final surrender to your newfound understanding of your soul path. All that has served your flesh understanding of life has been replaced by all that serves your soul understanding. Death to who you were and a birth to who you will be now.

The way you were is over, the way you will be is here. It's a new day and all things will be more meaningful, more intentional, you will be more observant. It is the catalyst for the remaining lessons.

Step 2: Desire

Prepare yourself for this transformation by wanting it. Embrace the peeling away of your humanness and the birth of your soul. Death is birth, and the next concept will prepare you for what is to come.

CONCEPT 14: TEMPERANCE

This is where you find peace in the journey, peace in that which you cannot or should not control. Here you will find in unwavering surrender. Rest for as long as it takes to gather the gumption to push forward. This is where it all stitches together. For some it will be a lifetime, for others, it will be instantaneous.

Remember, you just came out of the beginning stages of the death process and are about to walk into a deeper understanding of yourself, so breathe deeply and appreciate how far you've come. Gain your balance and gird up for what is coming next. Enjoy the peace in your soul.

Calm your elements - the mind, the emotions, the desires, and your sense of well-being - and just be still. Ask for guidance and follow your path step- by-step. This is where you practice what you have learned up to this point.

This is where you will rest until you are ready to carry forward. Take a deep breath and know that all is well.

CONCEPT 15:

COMING TO TERMS WITH YOUR FLESH

The attachments that restrict your growth will come front and center. The ultimate struggle is now underway, the struggle between the last strongholds of your flesh regarding the emerging soul. This is the final blow to the ego and the beginning of officially being in control of yourself. This lesson is the actual death of your humanness, not your body, but your attachment to the things that humanness deems important.

It's the last remaining contents of the box, way down at the bottom, the things you forgot to address already, the deep-buried aspects of your composition. That's why the previous lesson encouraged you to rest, pull it together, and wait... because this layer is the absolute most difficult concept to conquer... death to the ego a.k.a self-control.

Step 1: Examination

Here, you will begin to recognize the attachments that will restrict your growth. Attachments to the ego, and the human nature. All the foundations that you have built and every aspect of your life upon will be scrutinized and examined - by you.

Step 2: What You Don't See

This is where you will come to terms with the darker side of yourself, the side of yourself that you keep hidden from view. Uncomfortably exploring your shadow self, and often referred to as "dark night of the soul".

Everything that you are in denial about will come to the surface.

Escapism through various addictions, your understanding of the positive and negative energy exchange that comes with sex, your abusive or destructive personality traits, and all the toxic sticky mire of everything that your ego refuses to acknowledge will be exposed to you, and you will either recognize it as baggage and walk away, or you will stand here in a game of tug-of-war with the Universe... and it will hurt.

Step 3: Looking in The Mirror

Many people get stuck here. Many cannot accept or face the shadows that lurk deep inside. They simply do not move on because the feeding of the flesh-based ego at this foundational point is something they cannot function without. Staying stagnant in your deep depravity will send you straight back to Concept 1.

Here is where you finally let it all go, joyously let it all go and step into the next concept of your soul ascension.

CONCEPT 16:

SORTING THROUGH THE

RUBBLE AND REBUILDING

This concept represents the crumbling of an ideology because there is no longer a foundation to support it. With the realization of Lesson 15, with a final death blow to the ego, you will find yourself looking at the rubble of many situations, circumstances, and relationships that were built upon the old foundational understanding of your existence.

Step 1: Discomfort

You will no longer want to participate in the things that used to bring satisfaction to your ego because the ego no longer has control. You are no longer satisfied or entertained by the simplistic pleasures that used to please you. As a result, careers, relationships, living situations, etc. will fall by the wayside, permanently, once and for all.

Step 2: Learning to Just Simply Walk Away

The objective of this lesson is to know when to walk away. Walk away with the understanding that just because you've found your truth doesn't mean they have found theirs. Don't try to bring them/it with you, they are responsible for their own journey, and by now you will know in your understanding if these situations and circumstances are viable for your goal of growth and ascension. Just gracefully, compassionately, tactfully, walk away.

"Thank you for the journey, but my time here is over. There is not a foundation to build upon. I simply cannot create the life that I want for myself in this place. "

It is just that easy. If you are following your soul's guidance, the exit will appear, and you can just simply walk away. Remember, you have outgrown whatever this is in your life, and if you stay here against your intuition, your free will is choosing to deny your soul path. The direction towards your highest good comes from your intuition.

CONCEPT 17:

SEEING CLEARLY YOUR PATH AND YOUR PURPOSE

Coming out of Concept 16 opens the door for further understanding of your path and your purpose, and further revelation of your own personal "why". This is a time of renewal, refreshing, and focus. Here you find divine guidance for the next leg of your journey.

Step 1: Opportunities

Doors will open, people will appear, opportunities will present themselves, and the path will become crystal clear... all that you must do is recognize it AND step into it. It is here where you become open and agreeable to whatever it is that the universe sends your way, knowing definitively that it has been divinely orchestrated just for you according to the universal plan, and you are playing your part, administering your free will to follow where it leads you.

Step 2: Resistance Is Futile

Recognizing the path that is unfolding before you, and stepping onto it takes you exactly where you need to go, and at this level, the objective is to happily, willingly surrender to your calling, even when it doesn't match your expectations.

Chapter 16

Freedom

CONCEPT 18: ONE LAST PUSH

As the path and purpose of your life is revealed to you in the previous lesson, you will find yourself struggling between that which you know to be true in your guts, and that which you do not want to be your truth, because you may not agree with the direction of the universe.

For example, you may have spent your entire lifetime pursuing an education to achieve a professional goal, and your soul path is actually selling ice cream on a beach in Costa Rica because along that path you will plant seeds in the person who needs what only you have, or vice versa. Or, perhaps, you have dedicated your whole life to marriage and children, only to find out your spouse is the number one stumbling block to your growth, and your true purpose doesn't include them.

Maybe your religious training is now at odds with your spiritual growth, maybe you are outgrowing the fundamental beliefs engraved in your mind and you must now turn away from your culture and traditions to follow your soul's purpose in this lifetime. Not all of it is so drastic, but in this layer, you will be challenged to follow your soul's guidance despite your expectations, whatever they are.

Step 1: Surrender

This is the ultimate battleground, and this layer can be the Achilles Heel for every human, no matter the situation or the circumstances, no matter how far you've come in your quest for enlightenment. It is the ultimate struggle between the consciousness and the soul - the place where you will confront the ultimate human condition - the struggle between that which you know to be true in your intuition, and that which you do not want to accept as the truth in your mind.

Oftentimes, that which we know to be our truth, the knowing we feel in our guts, does not align with what our mind expects. Here is where you stop, once and for all, overriding the knowing you have inside of yourself. Here is where you will finally surrender everything to step into your true path and purpose.

Step 2: Checking Your Expectations at The Door

Remember the box analogy? Your mind is so trained on the target to be a viable, respectable, participating consumer, pursuing the expected path in line with all the other sheep that it is almost muscle memory to expect your ingrained expectations; and when you are faced with the real reality of anything different, growth suddenly becomes uncomfortable.

When you are faced with the crossroads of your future, it's hard to accept anything different than what you expected. "A spiritual awakening? Sure! I'll be the most spiritual (insert your expectations here) that there ever was!" sometimes turns into "Umm... you want me to do what??". When your true purpose turns out to be something other than what you thought it would be, many will fight against it. Remember, free will participation moves the universe.

Step 3: What is Your Truth?

This is the proving ground of your growth through all of the previous concepts, and a pivotal turning point in your desire to know and procure your life purpose. When you reach this point in your growth, will you truly recognize the truth that you know inside of yourself as your ancient soul speaking to your consciousness, and follow it wholeheartedly in the direction of your best and highest good. Will you draw a hard line in the sand and say, "This all stops here today" and follow your internal compass to your True North, no matter what, or will you continue to live in the box of your expectations?

Here is where you will find the truth of your commitment to your awakening.

CONCEPT 19: CLEAR VISION

When you successfully conquer the previous lesson, you will be securely set on the path to happiness, success, and vitality in your life. This lesson is not so much a stopping point, but a catalyst, because as you consciously chose your allegiance in the previous lesson, you enter into this lesson.

Choosing your soul's guidance over your human desire to have what you want, to get what you want; knowing internally that your soul is guiding you, catapults you into an elevated connection with Source. This puts you on the trajectory of living soulfully versus mechanically, of living by a higher frequency of consciousness vs low vibrational wants and desires.

Everything begins to unfold for you before your very eyes. Walking in a state of peace, knowing that you know... that your soul knows the better way.

CONCEPT 20: YOUR TRUTH

This is technically the last layer, as you will see when you get to the next concept, Concept 21. This is where you stand in power, achievement, and success, knowing who you are, how you got here, and where you are going. This is where you will combine all the steps of your growth to stand upon the foundation of your true self.

The true threads that you are sewn from, the strings of your soul that used to be layered under the tissues of your limited, boxed-in human understanding are now the ropes of your strength and the tether that will ground you to the ultimate end-game of soul ascension.

Upon your super- natural transition at death, your journey on this planet, in this lifetime, will have meaning and purpose to the next leg of your soul's journey in the beyond. Incorporating the soul's journey into your human experience leads you to your truth. Seek your true self, find your own truth, and your truth will set you free.

CONCEPT 21: THE END AND THE BEGINNING

Birth to death, death to birth. The old flesh-driven you is dead, and the new soul-guided you is born. This is the completion of your awakening and the beginning of the rest of your life. This concept closes out the initial awakening and creates the foundation for the next cycle of awakening. Transformative change and the expansion of one's horizons... that is exactly what is about to happen!

You will never look at life the same way again, you are elevated in your understanding of all things, and you are in a position to close out the long- standing cycle of living in the box. Here, you are now truly free. You will go from here straight back to the first concept to do it all again. However, this time you are ahead of the game, this time you have a foundation upon which to build.

This time, and next time, and the time after that... each new cycle builds upon the last, and each new cycle brings you closer and closer to accomplishing your life's purpose. Remember, the goal is spiritual growth, and any growth is an accomplishment. This is the last stop in your pursuit of your spiritual growth in this cycle of your life. This is where, through critical self-analysis, you step back and evaluate where you are and where you want to go, what you believe about who you are, and what you want from your experience here in this lifetime.

This is a time of congealing, solidification, reflection, and assessment of your past, and the creation of your focus for the future. This is where the previous cycle of your life comes to an end and the new phase of your life opens. These are the foundational stones by which you will experience all of the previous lessons again (and again and again), applying your personal growth, your spiritual growth, and your newfound vision of reality to your life.

This is the birth of the new you, in whatever varying degree of metamorphosis you have achieved. Life will be more beautiful, more colorful, much deeper, and peaceful.

Chapter 17

Closing Comments –

Where do you go from here?

As I said at the beginning of all this, this process is an ongoing tutorial, with layers to uncover, and goals to achieve. No one is going to go through these 21 concepts like classes at school, participating, testing, and then graduating with a diploma.

However, just like school, the lessons are layered upon each other, and elementary learning leads to advanced learning, and advanced learning, through many courses of study, eventually leads to mastery of the concepts - but there is always more to learn. You will return to concept one, but this time it will be easier to navigate because you already have the foundation in place to build upon. Concept after concept, layer after layer they will begin to intertwine in your life, and not necessarily in order this time.

This time around it will be more like spaghetti than waffles. Each new awakened perspective is a stone in the foundation of your life that you just keep building upon. You'll never have to go back to ground zero and till up the ground again, but you will have to keep building because there are infinite ways to learn. The more you learn, the more you grow. The more you grow, the stronger you become. Your strength dictates your ability to help humanity, one by one, awaken to a life of purpose, meaning, and peace.

Keep learning, keep weeding, and keep manicuring the landscape. If you stop taking care of the ground in your life, it will become overrun with weeds. Pull those weeds up when you see them starting to sprout, and keep your life weed-free. This is a new, fresh start with a new perspective by which to build a new understanding of how to live this crazy thing that we call life.

Go forth from here and apply what you have learned thus far in your journey to a fresh and new opportunity to live an easier existence and a better life.

A life with peace in your mind, peace in your emotions, peace in your desires, and peace in your well-being.

Know that there is purpose in the Universal order of things and that you are the threads that make up the tapestry of all things good. Follow your soul's guidance from this point forward and let it lead you and guide you deeper, and deeper, into your journey to the path that you were meant to walk in the true essence of who you are in your eternal soul.

Build upon the foundation that you have created through your awakening and know that you are important, and your life has meaning.

Enjoy the journey!

Namaste.

Epilogue

Now that you have made it through to the end of this book, the path is wide open for you to begin to create a beautiful life. Begin to live outside of the box, own your truth, the truth of the being you were meant to be.

Remember, you are a soul having a human experience, not a human having a soul experience. Let your ancient self guide you through your life and it will lead you to your path and your purpose in this lifetime.

Your intuition will always lead you to your best and highest good, even when you don't understand it. Follow it with peace in your soul and achieve great things for this life, and the next leg of your journey.

Afterword

I am a professional psychic medium who has gained the inspiration for this book through the 22 Major Arcana of the tarot cards. The ancient wisdom of these archetypes are the soul's guidance to maneuver the trials and tribulations of being alive in this human experience, and they offer spiritual wisdom to transform your journey. The tarot is not the tool of a "fortune teller", in the hands of an awakened and enlightened soul, they are the Guidestones for spiritual development.

Honestly, I have never even contemplated writing a book, let alone self-publishing a book. I am most certainly not a professional author, editor, typesetter, or publisher, but one day I had a vision of this book, and I simply disregarded it as a passing thought. Then, situations and circumstances manifested in my life, and signs and synchronicities appeared everywhere. I felt a movement inside of myself to just write, a throbbing "voice" in my guts to WRITE.

So, I did. I sat down and wrote for three days into the wee hours of the mornings, and four months later, after a self-taught crash course in how to write a book, here we are. It is my heartfelt wish that you live an amazing life. It is my mission and purpose to provoke you to think about things differently. To think about concepts that are important to your movement and growth.

Do what you will with it, take it or leave it. I've done what I was supposed to do, I have followed my soul's direction; and somehow, some way, this book plays an important part in my journey. I hope it sets the wheels in motion for you to embark upon yours.

Acknowledgment

Without the inspiration of my clients and the experiences that they have allowed me to be privy to, the subscribers to my YouTube channel, and the encouragement of my family and friends, this book would still reside in my mind.

Thank you to the friends who proofread and edited for me. I'm forever grateful for your support. Thank you all for believing in me.

About The Author

Dayna Marten is an international psychic spiritual advisor who uses her deep and innate understanding of the human psyche in unison with her potent spirituality to guide her clients toward their soul's purpose.

She is a powerful medium between your consciousness and your ancient self (your soul). Dayna teaches how to reconnect to your true north, to merge the human experience with the soul's mission, and walk the path of your best and highest good, according to Universal Order for your life.

Reference Guide to the
21 Levels of Spiritual Growth

Chapter 11 - Your Internal Life: The Three Concepts That Will Transform Your Journey

LEVEL 1 - GROUND ZERO (YOUR MIND)

Layer 1 - Taking Inventory

Layer 2 - What Are Your Assets?

Layer 3 - Prepping The Ground

Layer 4 - Planting The Seeds

LEVEL 2 - FOLLOWING THE VOICE WITHIN

Layer 1 - Finding Your True North

Layer 2 - Letting Go of Control

LEVEL 3 - THE INTEGRATION

Layer 1 - What Feels Right IS Right

Layer 2 - The Knowing

Made in United States
Troutdale, OR
12/13/2024